A CITY CALLED HEAVEN
(REVELATIONS 21 - 22)

G. BROWN-JOHNSON, C.O.T.K.

A CHILD OF THE KING

Additional Christian Education Reviewers:
Reverend Annie B. Darden, Author & Educator;
Reverend Lonnie Johnson, Pastor & Educator;
Dr. Phyllis J. Mayo, Psychologist & Educator.

This Book Belongs To

NAME

"A Child of the King"

- In God's time, Heaven is Made Just For You -

G. Brown-Johnson, C.O.T.K.

This Book is Dedicated
To All Children of the World.
Every Child that is a Believer

In God will one day soon and very soon,
Meet Face to Face
The King of Kings!

There is a land, not that far away beyond the clouds, and is to come,

"A City Called Heaven!"

You may have heard said, it is the Beautiful City of Zion and it is a City that is Great…!

The entrance of "A City Called Heaven" has the Glory of the King, and He is the Light, like a gem stone most precious, clear as crystal.

The wall of the City is so high, there is nothing that can ever climb over this wall.

Oh what a beautiful City.   "A City Called Heaven."

The entrance of "A City Called Heaven,"

also has Twelve Gates made of one Pearl:

On the East of "A City Called Heaven" are three gates;

On the North of "A City Called Heaven" are three gates;

On the South of "A City Called Heaven" are three gates;

On the West of "A City Called Heaven" are three gates.

There are names written on each of the Twelve Gates.

The names written on the Twelve Gates
are the Twelve tribes of a chosen nation, Israel.

Everyone enters through the Twelve Gates of this City.

The foundations of the wall look like the layers of a cake.
Each layer is beautiful and hard, but cannot be broken.

The foundations are made with the
most precious gem stones.

REUBEN SIMEON JUDAH ISSACHAR

ZEBULUN JOSEPH MANASSEH EPHRAIM

DAN ASHER NAPHTALI GAD

The Twelve names written on the Twelve Gates are:

Number One (#1): REUBEN – (rū – bĕn)

Number Two (#2): SIMEON – (sim é- on)

Number Three (#3): JUDAH – (jōō' – da)

Number Four (#4): ISSACHAR – (ĭs' ȧ – kȧr)

Number Five (#5): ZEBULUN – (zeb'yū - lūn)

Number Six (#6): JOSEPH – (jō – 'zĕf)

Number Seven (#7): MANASSEH – (mā – năs'ȧ)

Number Eight (#8): EPHRAIM – (ē 'frā – ĭm)

Number Nine (#9): DAN – (dă-n)

Number Ten (#10): ASHER – (ăsh'ĕr)

Number Eleven (#11): NAPHTALI – (năf ' tȧ - lí)

Number Twelve (#12): GAD – (gă – d)

The Bible says there are Twelve layers of precious stones –

One: Jasper – Onyx

Four: Emerald

Two: Sapphire - Ruby

Five: Sardonyx

Three: Chalcedony

Six: Sardius

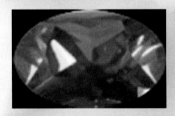

Which precious stone represents your birthday month?

_____

Seven: Chrysolite

Eight: Beryl

Nine: Topaz

Ten: Chrysoprasus

Eleven: Jacinth

Twelve: Amethyst

Which precious stone represents your birthday month?

_____

In "A City Called Heaven,"
is a pure river of water, the water of life,
clear as crystal, flowing from the throne of the King.

"A City Called Heaven," street is
pure Gold like a clear glass!

There is a tall and beautiful tree in
"A City Called Heaven."

On each side of the pure river of water is the Tree of Life
which has Twelve kinds of Fruit every month.

The Leaves on the tree are
not like any leaf ever seen.

The Leaves of the tree are for the
healing of the nations.

In "A City Called Heaven,"
there is no night, neither a light of the sun
for the King is the Light. His Light is for every one!

In "A City Called Heaven," it is filled with
clapping, dancing, and all believers are One family.

Lots of praising going on
and believers never get tired, in heaven.

Living in the Kingdom with the King, everyone is Happy!

Heaven is a City filled with Love
at all times and has many blessings!
In His Kingdom believers are in the presence of the King.
In His presence, we live free and do not want
for anything, living with the King!

It is the will of the King that all believers
will enter His Heavenly City.

All who enter are in Love with the King!

In this city there are so many Angels bowing down
and singing praises to the King!
The Angels are beautiful in "A City Called Heaven."
Can you Count the Angels?

How many Angels do you see? _____

This is how "heaven" is made. In the Beginning, the King of all the heaven, the earth, made everything that is made, and all that is seen.

In "A City Called Heaven," there is no sickness; there is no pain, and no dying. For in this City, there is no fighting, or guns that will kill. No one is ever hurt, because believers are now healed, living in His Kingdom, and in the presence of the King.

In "A City Called Heaven," the King with His Loving hands wipes all tears from every eye. There is nothing to be afraid of, have no fear, in "A City Called Heaven," there is no big bad Wolf!

Everyone is loving, sweet with compassion, and all things are New in "A City Called Heaven!"

While here on earth when entering
a place, there is a Door;

There is a knock at the door?

Someone on the other side of the door

will answer, allowing an entrance.

So it is with the King, an Open Door.

There is a knocking at the Door for every one…

Knock – Knock – Knock!

Who's there?

"The King!"

Open the Door and the King of Glory Shall Come in.

When the King comes in, not just the Twelve Gates, are open, the Windows of Heaven are also open!

The King pours out all Blessings flowing.

It rains so many showers upon whosoever will; for they shall enter His Kingdom.

When it is time, the King, is an Open Door in Heaven.

Believers in "A City Called Heaven" give praises
to the King because of what He has done
in order for believers to live in His Kingdom.

The King, the Beginning and the End (Alpha and Omega),
is worthy of all Glory and Honor
with Kingdom Authority.

He is the King, God the Son, born of a virgin,
Mary. Only the King gives, "Hope More Abundantly,"
in a dark world that had no light.

The King is called the "Lamb Worthy" who shed His Blood, in a dark place on a Cross at Calvary. He died on that Cross that believers may live In Him.

The King loves us so much!
He would not come down from that Cross,
but gave His life that everyone may live
and not die. In Him believers live forever.

His body was laid in a temporary space.

The King has all power and darkness

could not hold Him down because He is the Light!

He arose giving new life and returned to Heaven.

Because of what the King did, believers will enter
His Kingdom and live in "A City Called Heaven."

He promises to never leave any one.

Without a place to stay, in heaven, believers may live
with the King in His Kingdom.

Now He prepares a place where
believers will live and Praise Him forever.

The King shines the marvelous Light of His Glory
all around to every one with peace and happiness.

In "A City Called Heaven," believers walk in His Light.

His Light shines bright within each believer,

now "called" the Children of His Light!

"A City Called Heaven" is not made by Hand.

It will never pass away, this city is Everlasting!
The King rules the Kingdom and
makes everything right.

The King is in Heavenly places watching each of us.

He is coming back again for all believers!
Look to the sky. Every eye shall see Him.

His Words are the truth. He brought us
what was needed to enter His Kingdom.

A child of the King sits with Him in heavenly places.

In "A City Called Heaven," lives a Chosen
Generation; a royal priesthood; Chosen
by the King and is a Holy Nation.

Living in His Kingdom, "A City Called Heaven!"

Now walk together as children of the King.
No longer sad, but filled with His laughter!

In "A City Called Heaven"
believers are always in the presence of the King of Kings.

Humbly, bow down and Worship the King!
The King Reigns Forever and Ever.

Oh, What a beautiful City!
That beautiful City is:

"A City Called Heaven!"

(Revelations 21 – 22) - Sing together…

Oh, what a beautiful city (repeat 3 times)
Twelve gates to the city, Hallelujah!
Say it is oh, what a beautiful city
Oh, YES Lord, what a beautiful city
Twelve gates to the city, Hallelujah!

There are three gates in the East!
There are three gates in the West!
There are three gates in the North!
There are three gates in the South!

That makes Twelve gates to the city, Hallelujah!
And it is oh, what a beautiful Oh
Yes my Lord, OH, what a beautiful city
Twelve gates to the city, Hallelujah!
Oh What a Beautiful City!

All Believers in the King may enter

"A City Called Heaven!"

Remember: Believers must now prepare and "Be Ready!"

The King will very quickly come with a shout:

"IT IS TIME TO ENTER!"

Whosoever, Believes in Him

has Everlasting Life!

Now by Faith, Believe His Word is, True, and the King is

J – E – S – U – S!

In "A CITY CALLED HEAVEN!" –

"The Lord Is There, and Is Everywhere!"

† Appreciation †

All Praises to God,
the Power of
His Holy Spirit,

The Holy Bible – (Revelations 21-22)

"In A City Called Heaven,"

"Crown HIM Lord of Lords!"

ORDER FORM

Xlibris

Xlibris Corporation
1-888-795-4274
www.Xlibris.com
Orders@Xlibris.com

4 Ways to Order:

- Postal Orders: Mail to the Address above:

- EMAIL: gbjcotk@gmail.com

- MAIL FORM TO: P. O. Box 1918, Clinton, MD 20735

- Fax: To send this form by fax -- NOTE: email first to E-mail Address

Item	Unit Cost	QTY	TOTAL
"A CITY CALLED HEAVEN"			
Maryland Sales Tax			
Shipping & Handling (USA) -- per book)			
(Canada -- S & H per book; International - S & H per book)			
TOTAL			

Forms of payment:

Check: payable to: Child of the King, P. O. Box 1918, Clinton, MD 20735

Credit Card: [ ] VISA   [ ] Master Card   [ ] Discover   [ ] American Express

Card #: _____   Exp. Date: _____

Name on Card: _____   Address: _____

City, State, Zip _____

Ship to:

Name _____

Address _____

City, State, Zip _____

Printed in the United States
By Bookmasters